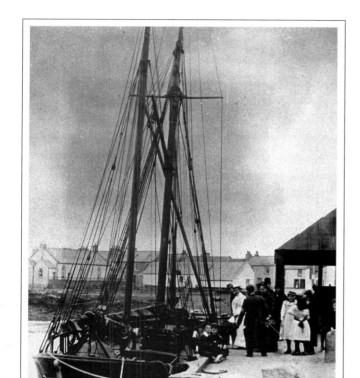

Dumfries and

Through the Lens
Glimpses of old
Galloway Seaports

Dumfries and Galloway Libraries,
Information and Archives
with Whithorn Photographic Group
2000

First published 2000
© Publication copyright Dumfries and Galloway Council.
Text copyright Whithorn Photographic Group.

Designed by Dumfries and Galloway Libraries, Information
and Archives. Set and printed by Solway Offset Services,
Catherinefield Industrial Estate, Dumfries for the publisher.

Dumfries and Galloway Libraries, Information and Archives
Central Support Unit, Catherine Street
Dumfries DG1 1JB

ISBN 0946280 47 9
Galloway Seaports is number 18 in the
Dumfries and Galloway: Through the Lens series.
For a full list of our publications write to the above address.

ACKNOWLEDGEMENTS

Mrs. Jaques, Mrs. Sayers, Miss Donaldson, Mr. B.
Brown, Mrs. McWilliam, Mrs. R. Cameron, Mr. J.
Niblock, Mrs. S. McGuire, Mrs. Topping, Mr. J.
Campbell, Mr. A. Gladstone, Dr. G. Brown, Mrs.
Gibson, Mrs. Kiltie, Mrs. E. Ker, Mrs. Blain, Mr.
W. King-Webster, Mr. J. Scoular, Mr. J. Leather,
Mrs. J. Evans, Mr. D. Nelson, Dumfries and
Galloway Museums, Dumfries and Galloway
Libraries, Information and Archives, and Scottish
Media Group newspapers (for permission to
reproduce the picture of salmon stake-netting).

PREFACE

I am privileged to have been asked to write the preface of this book. I have read the text, and the detail of the historical and geographical facts, which has been so carefully researched on the fishing industry in South West Scotland, is fascinating reading. However the main reason for wishing this book to sell well is because the profit of the sale of this book is to be donated to the Memorial Fund of the *Solway Harvester*.

Some years ago, I had the honour to become the Patron of *The Mallaig and North West Fisherman's Association*. Through this association I have learnt some of the problems of the current fishing industry, and also shared the joys and sorrows of fishermen and their families in many parts of Scotland. I have great respect for the dignity and courage of many folk, who have had to face awesome tragedy and profound sadness.

I wish this book success, and I hope that many will buy it and enjoy it, and also remember seven, fine young men who died at sea in January, 2000.

Frances Shand Kydd

INTRODUCTION

Looking at a modern road-map, it would be easy to see Galloway as a geographical area isolated from the central belt of Scotland and the world of commerce by the mass of the Southern Uplands. Every fisherman and seafarer in Galloway knows, however, that it is in fact part of a quite different and entirely sea-borne world of communications: the small circle of the Irish Sea, through which it is intimately linked to Ireland, Man, Cumbria and Liverpool. The apparent dominance of the road is only the result of a foreshortened historical perspective: until comparatively recently, it was far easier and more economic to send goods to Whitehaven from Drummore by sea than to attempt an overland journey.

With its long indented coastline and river estuaries, its warmer inshore waters and cold, deeper waters, its characteristically fast tidal race and shifting sand-bars, the western Solway has had a culture and economy of the sea for hundreds – indeed, for thousands – of years. These have left us with a rich heritage of buildings and harbours, of vessels built and adapted for the special conditions and purposes of the Solway, and of human tradition and skill, which we attempt to record here.

It is hard for the land-lubber not to be impressed at the sheer assurance with which the seafarer handled the complexities of a different and unpredictable world: the geography of the Solway, the moods of the sea, the riches of its hidden life and its opportunities. Those used to thinking in terms of the dull uniformities of trawlers and factory ships will find here a bewildering variety of tackle, technique and craft employed to catch fish – yairs, haaf-nets, flounder and salmon stake-nets, long-lines – with barques, sloops, shrimpers, paddle-steamers, steam-drifters and oyster-smacks used to cross or harvest the sea. That this variety grows out of long development is attested by physical remains and historical documents: a Charter of 1511 confirms a previous grant to Whithorn of a port, its rights and duties, at the Isle; seventeenth century witnesses describe obviously well-established fishing practices and levels of coastal trade. This book is intended as a celebration and a record of that tradition, and of the men and women who produced and lived it.

As usual, my colleagues and friends Lesley Murray, Joe Whiteford and Jim Allan have contributed images, information, time and hard work. John Scoular, Jack Niblock, Guy Brown and Brian Perks by giving freely of their seafaring knowledge and understanding of the history of the Solway have contributed substantially to the preparation of the book.

Julia H Muir Watt,
Whithorn Photographic Group   September 2000

Isle of Whithorn from the Cairn

This view of the Isle shows a top-sail schooner lying at the coaling berth, next to the open shed. The white-coloured buildings were grain stores, first owned by Mr Duff of Whithorn, then by Wyllie's grain merchants. During the Second World War they were used as a canteen by the WVS. In the foreground is the boat park, at the entrance to the Cairn. The profile of Tonderghie Row has altered little, except for one or two houses which have been built up to two storey height, and Bysbie Mill, which can be glimpsed, still standing and in operation, just adjacent to the mast of the Schooner

Isle Quay

Taken on the same day as the view from the Cairn, this picture gives a full view of the warehouses, with blocks and tackle at attic level, and granaries along the quay. The right to construct and operate a harbour was confirmed in the Charter granted by James IV to the Priory of Whithorn in the sixteenth century. The current quay dates from 1790, when the true island of the Isle was joined to the mainland; the right-angled extension was added in the nineteenth and twentieth centuries. Next to the Stores, what now forms part of the *Steam Packet Hotel* is here still a private house, but the *Steam Packet* was already in existence and can be glimpsed on the extreme left of the picture. Its first landlord was a ship's carpenter, Geordie Hannah, who died in 1896 and was said to be the last of the wooden ship-builders. He was followed as landlord by Mr McVey, assisted by Miss Margaret Reid, who kept the inn until 1907, and then was succeeded by Jimmy Robertson. A local fishing smack lies in front of the hotel.

Isle of Whithorn: Fishermen's Cottages, 1880s

The row of fishermen's cottages is longer in the picture than it appears today: then, there was a smiddy and a pony-and-trap house close to the road. On the other side of the road, the low white building was a sty for the miller's pigs; the ventilator on the kiln of Bysbie Mill appears prominently above the whitewashed cottages on the right and survived into the 1940s. The miller's pigs, as one resident remembers, living adjacent to the burn and the sea, were sometimes fed on an unusual diet of live eels. To the extreme left of the row of cottages, a barn, now demolished, stands in the field.

Oyster Smacks, Isle of Whithorn, 1880s

The existence of oysters in Luce Bay, and also in the waters of Loch Ryan at Kirkcolm had been acknowledged since the seventeenth century: Andrew Symson, in 1684, describes the gathering of oysters off the *Skares* in Kirkcolm parish. The nineteenth century saw the development of a significant oyster-dredging industry in Essex and this important photograph documents the presence of large Colne smacks at the Isle of Whithorn in the 1880s. The success of the Essex oyster fishery, based largely at the villages of Wivenhoe, Rowhedge and Brightlingsea, had stimulated the local development and building of the large rakish cutters seen in the picture. These cutters pursued oyster and scallop fishing as far afield as the Channel Islands and Wales as well as in the Solway Firth. They were equipped with a hand-spike anchor windlass, a four-barrelled hand winch for working halyards and running out the bowsprit, and a hand-operated winch or capstan amidships for working the dredge. One can only imagine the effort of pulling in the sea-dredges, which were equipped with hoeing edges like a harrow, from deep water. Fifty of these large professional craft were active in the Solway Firth during the 1880s. It is still possible to trace Essex names at the Isle of Whithorn.

Countess of Galloway Under Steam *(previous page)*
This impressive view of the Isle shows the second paddle steamer to be given the name *Countess of Galloway:* this one was iron-built, replacing a wooden vessel built in 1835. The *Free Press* of 1846 described the launch from the yards of Todd and McGregor on the Clyde of *a splendid new iron steamship for the Galloway and Liverpool trade. She was gaily decked with flags, and amid the cheers of the assembled crowd, took the water in a capital style.* The ship had cost £16,000 was owned in Wigtown by the Galloway Steam Navigation Company. She operated mainly from Kirkcudbright, the Isle and Garlieston, with occasional trips to Port William, carrying both cargo, particularly cattle and sheep, and passengers. She had a gross tonnage of 451 tons, and in 1872 a passage from Garlieston to Liverpool took ten hours. On occasion, she undertook longer journeys, travelling as far as Scrabster, Caithness in 1874, bringing home, under the guidance of Captain Bowes, a cargo of 1,800 sheep, of which a remarkable 1,799 survived the long journey. The railways were by this time already threatening her dominance over cargo trade, and in the late 1870s, she was sold, and was used largely between Stranraer and Liverpool. By 1880 she had been broken up at Port Glasgow.

Ship Built at the Isle *(facing page)*
This three-masted barque, built at the Isle, represents important evidence of a now vanished part of its history: it is thought that the ship-building tradition reaches back to the close of the eighteenth century, when a Mr Broadfoot constructed a ship called the *Cutcloy.* He was succeeded by Peter McMeeking who was still in business in 1852, by which time he had been joined in the trade by William McWilliam, the first of the famous Isle ship-builders. The first ship to be completely constructed by a McWilliam was the schooner *Comet,* of fifty tons, skippered by Captain A Brodie, an Isle man. Others were skippered by the McWilliams themselves, who carried out the shipbuilding business in the part of the Isle known as the *Old Haw Port.* The saw-pits can still be traced where the petrol pumps are now. The narrow street passing up the side of the Wigtown Bay Sailing Club's clubhouse was known as *Jiboom Street* since the bows of the boats reached there; beyond that, there was a timber-yard. It was their first three-masted ship, the *Wigtownshire,* built in 1860, which we may presume is the one in the picture, which caused the demise of the McWilliam ship-building business: a cargo of machinery headed for Buenos Aires was supplemented by a cargo of salt, which, by the end of the long journey, had corroded the valuable machines. It was at this point that the McWilliams built their famous shop – using immense left-over ship's-timbers – at the head of their patent slipway. The slipway was later dismantled and taken to Carrickfergus.

After the Storm, Isle of Whithorn 1964
A memorable night in Isle history occurred in 1964 when a spring-tide only retreated half-way out into the bay, and, at high-tide, rushed back into the village after midnight. Those who saw the ominous signs the preceding evening had stowed boats here, in Jiboom Street, for protection, but this did not prevent the sea pouring through McWilliam's shop. It also left a tide-mark two feet up the walls of houses on Main Street. The Standard Eight car, in the picture, had been washed up and down the street several times.

Hauling in the Lifeboat, Isle of Whithorn

The large number of men hauling the life-boat on its launching carriage back into its house shows the considerable effort it must have been to pull it up the slope from the water by hand. Nonetheless, the position of the station offered considerable natural advantages, allowing a launch to either Wigtown or Luce Bay, as weather and distress calls demanded. The lifeboat is the characteristic *self-righting* type, introduced in the mid-nineteenth century, with high air-cases at either end enabling it to right itself in the event of a capsize. The lifeboat house was also of a standard design, approved by the RNLI. The volunteer crew, of at least ten men, would have rowed the boat, and were equipped with cork life-vests. The Isle of Whithorn station was founded in 1868, and the *Charlie Peek* was its first lifeboat, from 1869-1886. In 1886, a Miss Leighton donated a new lifeboat, and it was pulled from Whithorn, amid scenes of great civic excitement, by nine horses. It was named the *John and Henry Leighton,* and was replaced by the *George and Margaret* in 1901. In 1919, the entire station was closed and replaced by a motor-powered boat operating from Kirkcudbright.

Main Street, Isle of Whithorn

This picture of the lifeboat progressing in what seems radically the wrong direction up Main Street, pulled by the two cart-horses, seems to provide a puzzle, since it is leaving the harbour behind it. The lifeboat, however, could be launched from Cairnhead, if either the weather was unfavourable at the Isle, or if the distressed ship was located well into Wigtown Bay. It is possible to note that the farm gates at Cairnhead are still wider than average, being built to accommodate the lifeboat, and that there is a granite pillar to catch the bogie as it swung round. It is scarcely possible to imagine, in today's world of split-second responses, what delays such a slow process might have entailed, but it was common for the self-righting boats to be taken to convenient launching points by land, both because they were light enough to be launched from an open beach, and because rowing against the wind to a distant casualty was even slower and more exhausting work.

Black Huts, Monreith Bay

Until recently, the *black huts* were a familiar sight at The Lag, Monreith, where they were conveniently positioned for the seasonal lobster fishing. The first family to establish a fishing station here came from the Rhins; they were followed by Charlie McGuire from the Isle, who had permission from Sir Herbert Maxwell to fish from the foreshore and lived here for the summers for nearly fifty years. At this time, there might have been between four to six boats operating from this point. The presence of three huts in the photograph dates it to a period prior to the 1930s, when one was demolished; the remaining huts survived until the 1990s. The lobsters were brought to Whithorn station, and then transferred to the *Paddy* at Newton Stewart, for London markets. In reminiscences given to guests at his 84th birthday, Charlie McGuire remembered his biggest-ever lobster, weighing 16½lbs., which he reckoned was 300 years old and tasted like limestone; he sold it as a curiosity to a gentleman from Liverpool. Charlie had one further connection with the Maxwell family: he advised Gavin Maxwell that, to obtain eels for his pet otters, he should tie a bag of oat-straw to a pipe underwater. The experiment was wholly successful and obtained the otters' food-supply for a week.

13

Isle Regatta, 1920s

With so many seafaring families at the Isle, regattas had been popular summer sport since 1861 and continued into the 1930s when a tragic accident occurred during a race. The regattas resumed after World War II. The local fishing boat in the foreground is being used by spectators, or possibly judges, while behind it, at the coal berth, lies the steamer *Hamilton*. There was a weigh-bridge at this point on the quay; the open shelter by the coal berths, seen in other pictures, has by this time been demolished. We can glimpse a front view of the whitewashed stores behind, now belonging to Wyllie's grain business, and stabling to the right.

Garlieston Harbour

Beside the schooner lying at berth are goods wagons of the Glasgow and South Western Railway loaded with timber. The original railway terminus had been at Millisle, but once the line to Whithorn opened in 1877, a new station was built for Garlieston village and the line continued from the station right into the harbour. For a time the railways lived alongside the coastal trade and did not, at least at Garlieston, spell its immediate demise. The crane beyond the wagons would have been used for lifting heavy loads; beyond lies a local fishing vessel.

Arrival of Steamers, Douglas, Isle of Man
A typical scene of the arrival of tourists at Douglas from the steamers, where they are being met by horse-drawn cabs and horse-drawn trolleys. The annual paddle steamer trips from Garlieston to Douglas and the island were already proving popular in 1892, when the *Free Press* reported that over one thousand people, some from Newton Stewart and some from Whithorn, converged on Garlieston to board the *Snaefell* for a day-trip. In the small world of the Irish Sea, however, trading and other links between Wigtownshire and Man, only sixteen miles distant, are inevitably very much older. Whithorn Priory had subsidiary churches on Man, and, most famously, the island was the source of the duty-free goods which were smuggled to the Galloway coast, until the Isle of Man was bought from the Duke of Atholl by the British Government in 1830.

Ship Building at Garlieston

If this scene of ship-building at Garlieston does not make it look like a major industry, it certainly must have been so earlier in the nineteenth century: from about 1800, sloops were built here, often named after the Earl of Galloway's family: the *Lady Mary Stewart* of 100 tons was built in 1862, the *Keith Stewart* (named after a popular comrade of Lord Nelson's) as far back as 1818. By 1852 in Garlieston, there were two master-mariners – William Hannah and James Dunsmore, a tide-waiter, and William Marshall, ship-owner and timber merchant. In fact, in 1854, a reporter on the *Free Press* could assume, when speaking of Hannah's shipyard at Garlieston, that *Mr Hannay's* [sic] *character and success as a ship-builder are now too well-known to require special notice.* The pier and harbour were built in 1816, with a rubble pier in 1838, and an extension in 1855. The Dumbie breakwater was constructed in 1843. Rope and sail-cloth were manufactured along the north-west of the bay and Garlieston was, of course, a port of call for the *Countess of Galloway.*

Garlieston with Herring Fleet

Judging from the profile of the coaster in the background, the date of this photograph is probably in the late 1950s, or possibly the early 60s, when the herring fleet, this one possibly consisting of Irish boats, had landed at Garlieston. In fact, by the 1950s, an official report commented that landings of herring were largely not made by local boats. Of course, by this time, the herring boats were motorised. This photograph, no doubt taken from one of the windows in the grain mill overlooking the harbour, shows clearly the pier and its extension.

Wigtown Harbour

Wigtown's first harbour, captured in the well-known aquatint by William Daniell in 1815, was to the north of the present harbour, and would have been approached roughly at the point where the car park for the Martyr's Stake is now placed. The new harbour was built as a response to a natural change in the course of the Bladnoch river; the old harbour silted up rapidly after its successor was opened in 1818. Neither harbour had elaborate harbour-works and consisted of a simple quay, built of rubble and wood. The apparent desertion of the harbour in this picture belies a more lively past: the small rectangular basin, where the boat is berthed in this picture, was used to turn the *Countess of Galloway* steamship when she came into dock. The harbour could take vessels of up to 300 tons and there was also a full staff of customs officers and some ship-building at Wigtown from the early nineteenth century. Here the photographer has used the boat which ferried him across, and its occupants, to present a balanced composition and a view of the town from an unusual angle. The railway line, positioned just close to the harbour, can be seen running along the cut parallel to the water; the station would have been to the left of the picture.

Flounder Fishing, Wigtown

This evocative picture of Wigtown Bay shows Robert McGuffie, to the left, carrying the fish, and his partner with the flounder they have caught in the nets. Catching fish by means of static traps, in which they were stranded by the movements of the tide, has a long history on the Solway: the mouth of the Luce river still shows traces of dry stone dykes or weirs, which would have been extended by wattle screens and were supposed to have been built by the monks at the Abbey of Glenluce; *cruives* also existed on the Cree near Castle Stewart. Less glamorous and highly developed than the parallel industry of salmon stake-netting, flounder fishing was nonetheless a regulated activity, with certain areas designated for each fisherman. The nets were smaller and less complex than the labyrinths of the salmon stake-nets, and would no doubt have trapped a variety of white fish. Probably, however, the industry was not sufficiently developed for export and the fish were only sold locally on the streets of Wigtown. Robert McGuffie was brother to Louis McGuffie, VC, hero of World War I, but had himself been wounded in action in 1918, when his left arm had to be amputated.

Stake-Nets, Wigtown Bay

The salmon stake-nets are a familiar and characteristic sight on the shores of Wigtown Bay. They are the visible sign of a highly regulated industry, in which both sites and fishing equipment are formally controlled. The stakes, up to 20 feet in length, support nets, which are designed to intercept salmon and sea-trout on their migrations, and which therefore consist of barriers variously angled towards the tide, and of pockets into which the fish are then diverted and from which they cannot escape. There is a close-season from the end of August until early February, and during the season, there is a weekly close-time all weekend. Setting nets at the beginning of the season, collecting the catch, repairing nets, and off-season maintenance work was a labour-intensive activity, which, even now with the introduction of tractors to haul nets, and of artificial fibres which do not require conservation by traditional tarring, still requires highly specialised tools and remains in many respects manual and traditional. Here a fisherman gives a final blow to a captured salmon with a club.

Haaf-Netting on the Solway

Haaf-netting seems to require more than usual courage and fortitude from the fishermen involved: a row of men, up to eight or nine, stand chest-deep in the fast running tides of the Solway estuaries. Despite the danger, the outermost stance is sought after, no doubt because of the increased chances of trapping salmon in the deeper water, and lots are drawn as to who should take this position. Families were often engaged in this type of fishing from one generation to another. The men stand in a slanting row, each holding a *poke* net slung from a cross-bar and supported at either end by a pole; the nets are swung upwards and over the bar once a fish was detected, so sealing the pocket. The men wear long waders, carry a sack for the catch and a club to kill the fish. Areas with large stretches of flat sand are the most favoured places for this type of fishing, and although this practice only survives in the eastern Solway, on the Nith and Annan, licences for this type of fishing existed as far west as the Cree and an early description of *half-netting* [sic] by Andrew Symson in the 1690s gives a detailed description of the practice as carried out on the sands of Baldoon, near Wigtown. *Haaf* is the Norse word for *ocean*, but in the Northern Isles the word is used to refer to a quite different sort of fishing, using a long line from small boats far out to sea.

Creetown

This maritime view of Creetown and its harbour at high-water reminds us that, before the advent of the bypass road and of land reclamation, the origins of the settlement were intimately connected with the sea. As the *Ferrytown of Cree*, it had been the point where pilgrims on their way to Whithorn were given hospitality for the night and were ferried across Wigtown Bay, and throughout the nineteenth century, we may read of daily passage boats to Wigtown. It became a focus for English fishing families, who were migrating from the south and settling on the Solway, and some of these, such as the Birrell brothers, played a significant part in the development of the salmon stake-netting industry, which is still in evidence at Creetown and Carsluith. The vessel in the picture is thought to be an early form of shrimping boat; these have now become rare sights on the Solway, but were once common. They trawled the sea-bed, forcing the shrimp into a fine-meshed net; the shrimp were then sieved, tipped into a basket and boiled on board.

23

Gatehouse of Fleet

The Gatehouse bypass road has obscured the connection between the burgh and its harbour, but the berthed top-sail schooner here reminds us that the Fleet was navigable for relatively large vessels. This is Port McAdam, which replaced an earlier harbour at Boat Green, which continued to have boat-building and repair yards until the middle of the nineteenth century. *Pigot's Directory* for 1852 explains how Mr Murray had cut a canal to deepen the river at a cost of £3000, and how since then, Mr McAdam had constructed a *commodious quay... and received the thanks of the ships owners of Kirkcudbright for his spirited enterprise, by which their shipping has been so greatly benefitted* [sic]. The quay was dry-stone, with a timber-front construction, which can be glimpsed in the picture. Gatehouse was then exporting grain and importing lime and coal. The proximity of Gatehouse to numerous smuggling haunts along the coast, including the famous cave known, after Scott, as *Dirk Hatteraick's,* reminds us that the heavily indented coastline, with its numerous landing places and places of concealment, was perfect for the contraband trade, as well as more legitimate trading activities.

Yair-Netting at Kirkcudbright

Various traditional methods of catching salmon in the estuaries take advantage of the rapid tidal flow of the Solway, which leaves behind it pools and channels in which fish are naturally trapped. The method employed on the Dee, and also at one time near Creetown, was the *yair*. As can be seen from the photograph, the fisherman worked the net from a scaffold on which he sat, while below him there was a V-shaped enclosure made of wattle, into which the salmon swam with the tide. The strings attached to the net were sensitive to its movements and alerted the fisherman above to the presence of his catch. Families involved with yair and lobster fishing at Kirkcudbright included the Stitts, Parkhills, Polands and Gourlays.

Kirkcudbright Harbour *(facing page)*

The dominance of Kirkcudbright as one of the main fishing ports in Galloway, as well as the main lifeboat station, is a largely post World War II development, particularly connected with the growth of the *queenie* or scallop fishing industry. In this picture, taken probably at the end of the nineteenth century, one can see how the river had crucially influenced the development of the burgh for many centuries. To the left of the picture, what is now the harbour car park was once the site of a boat dock, constructed in the early nineteenth century on a tidal creek of the river. At one point, the river and marshes almost encircled the High Street, which must have given it a much more maritime aspect than it now appears to have. *Slater's Directory* of 1852 certainly gives a picture of a burgh in which seafaring played a great part: nine ship-owners are mentioned, as well as Stitt and Campbell, ship-builders, a harbour-master and customs-officer. The ruins of McLellan's Castle look rather unfamiliar here, clad in ivy.

Lobster Creels, Kirkcudbright Harbour *(following page)*

This small building appears in the previous photograph, adjoining the building which is now the Harbour Gallery. A triangular doo-cot is built into the gable of what was then a row of fishermen's cottages. The lobster fisherman in the centre of the picture was Adam Leckie. There is little change in the design of the creels from the time of this photograph to the present day, although the frames would have been made of cane, rather than of aluminium or plastic tubing, and the weights to sink the pots were probably stone, rather than concrete. The boat in the extreme foreground is probably the rowed craft which was used for potting, and it might have taken up to four men to row and haul in the creels. The pots were let down on a single line, and, at this time, there would have been no form of winch to wind in the rope.

Port William Harbour, 1870s

Well before the settlement planned by Sir William Maxwell, there had been a fishing settlement at the mouth of the Killantrae Burn. The harbour took thirty years to build being completed in the 1790s. The pier was extended before the middle of the nineteenth century. This photograph was taken before the harbour was reconstructed and the basin widened by the Maxwells in the late 1890s to mark the Diamond Jubilee. The Maxwells had encouraged shipbuilding at the Port in the early nineteenth century: the vessels included one, the Dirk Hatteraick, a sloop of 47 tons built in 1818. The reference to the famous smuggler was apposite for Port William where the illegal activities in the hinterlands of Mochrum Parish were so blatant that a military barracks and customs post was established in the Port in 1788 to control the menace.

The Ellen and Mary

Both the schooner in the picture, with its handsome figure-head, and the face of its Master, David McGuffie, would have been familiar sights on the Solway, and particularly at Port William. The vessel was built at Garlieston by Messrs. Hannah in 1868, and was owned by the Routledge family until Messrs. James Wyllie bought out the feeding and grain businesses from them, together with the ship. David McGuffie was her captain for thirty years, which created a record on the Solway. The usual cargos, carried between Whitehaven, Maryport and Belfast were coal (up to 80 tons of it), manures and feeding stuffs. Later in her career, she had an engine installed, but by 1936, her condition was such that she failed a Board of Trade inspection and was broken up on King's Green at Port William by David McGuffie, her last master. As a local poem laments: *the Ellen and Mary has finished her wandering. And the ports of the Solway shall know her no more.*

Captain John Hill, Port William

Captain John Hill (1829-1902) was one of a dynasty of sea-captains, in a profession which seemed to be hereditary. His father and his grandfather, both named Alexander Hill, were captains. A poem exists in honour of his grandfather, who died in 1816. In Port William as elsewhere in the Machars, the same names occur again and again in connection with seafaring and its peripheral businesses – as captains, entrepreneurs, owners and sometimes builders: the Routledges, Gibsons, MacQueens and Hills are just some examples. Here, Captain Hill appears in the uniform and cap-badge of the Manx Steamship Company, of which he became Commodore of the fleet of steamships. Earlier in his career, he was master of the coastal trader *Ann Musgrave* in the 1870s, carrying the characteristic cargos of manure, coal and animal feed up and down the Solway, and owner of the sloop *Barganny,* whose master was another Alexander Hill, probably John Hill's brother.

Stairhaven

Stairhaven, was built, as its name suggests, by the Earl of Stair, in the 1840s and later improved in the 1890s. Then, as now, the pier looks rather incongruous, given the size of the village. Its sheltered harbour was used in the nineteenth century for loading and unloading heavy cargoes, such as lime and manures. It had been the site of some smuggling activity, and had its own salmon fishing station whose appointed area extended along the coast from St. Helena Island to Ringdoo Point, and to just south of the quay. Even in the 1950s, two men were employed here for the salmon fishing season, and the proprietor eked out the winter by gathering shell-fish. The fish were shipped by rail from Glenluce, to either Glasgow or London.

Drummore Harbour

The impressive array of carts in the picture is waiting to load cargo from the puffer *Hamilton,* which is delivering coal from Maryport. The coaster was owned by J. Marshall and Sons of Drummore, and her master was J. McCorquodale; she ceased trading in 1929 and was laid up. The pier at Drummore was built in 1845, and later extended in 1889, before this photograph was taken. On the whole, Drummore's coastal trade lasted longer than that of other ports, since the railway never extended south of Portpatrick and the sea remained the obvious route for heavy goods such as coal and feeding stuffs. The boat in the foreground is a double-ended fishing-boat.

Schooners at Drummore

These top-sailed schooners, for all their air of elegance, were the work-horses of the Solway from the middle of the nineteenth century, some keeping up the coastal trade between the Wigtownshire ports, Ireland, Whitehaven, Maryport and Liverpool until the Second World War. The name *Mayflower* may be read on the bow of the first vessel; she had originally been a Belfast ship, but was transferred to Stranraer in 1896. Many of these schooners were locally built, owned and mastered.

Mull of Galloway Lighthouse
The southernmost tip of Scotland at the Mull has always been a favourite destination for outings, as here with Kirkmaiden United Free Sunday School, which has come up the long and winding road in farm carts. In fact, the lighthouse warns shipping of the dangerous tidal race below the point of the peninsula. Many small boats preferred to avoid the race by pulling their craft over-land at the boat-haul naturally formed by the narrow isthmus just north of the Mull. The lighthouse was built in 1828-30 to the design of Robert Stevenson, who provided a projecting walkway round the lantern, with stores and keepers' houses at the base.

Port Logan Lighthouse and Quay

Port Logan, like some of the other harbours – such as that at Stairhaven in the Machars — was built by an ambitious laird wishing to develop his estates and, like the others, never quite lived up to its founder's ambitions. Port Logan, or Port Nessock, at least had the prospect of rivalling Portpatrick as a terminus for Irish traffic, and Colonel Andrew McDouall of Logan commissioned a report from the distinguished engineer, John Rennie, in 1813. The harbour was actually built in 1818-20, under the superintendence of John Young. The pier is built ruggedly of ashlar blocks and the lighthouse itself, dated 1830, looks sturdily different from a Stevenson construction. It is interesting to speculate how the ogee-topped light-chamber was actually lit. On the ground floor, there is a room with a fireplace, and beneath the outside stair, there is an intriguingly two-seatered latrine, with mural chute.

Portpatrick Harbour

The engineering history of Portpatrick harbour is a complex one, owing to the difficulties of protecting the inner harbour from the ravages of the sea beyond. It was the earliest port to develop connections with Ireland and with Donaghadee in particular, and its black cattle trade in the seventeenth century. Portpatrick's monopoly of cross-channel traffic appeared to be sealed with the introduction of a daily mail service, and with its potential for transporting troops quickly to Ireland, after the construction of the military road in 1765. The harbour itself, remained almost without harbour works until the end of the eighteenth century, when John Smeaton put forward a scheme for a north and south harbour, protected by piers and bulwarks. The sea destroyed the north pier in 1801, and a proposal by John Rennie twenty years later ended with the destruction of the south pier by a hurricane in 1836. If the power of the sea was one difficulty, the trailing clouds of steam left by the *Paddy* in our picture gives a clue to the real cause of Portpatrick's demise: despite the construction in 1865 of a larger rectangular basin to accommodate the steam-boats by then used by the Royal Mail, these could just as easily travel into the calmer waters of Loch Ryan. By 1868, only three years later, the ferry service was officially transferred to Stranraer.

Corsewall Lighthouse

Corsewall was built in 1815-16, the first light to be lit in a programme of lighthouse-building by the Northern Lighthouse Board under the benevolent dictatorship of Robert Stevenson. He was the founder of a dynasty of lighthouse-builders, of whom the least successful apprentice was his grandson, Robert Louis Stevenson. The oil-burning lamp with its twelve reflectors was apparently so effective that daytime covers had to be provided to prevent spontaneous combustion. There is a walkway at the lowest stage and quatrefoil decoration at the top. The keepers' cottages were built at the same time. The photographer has ensured interest in the distance by taking in the passing paddle-steamer. Corsewall was automated, like all other lighthouses in Britain, in the 1990s, and the accommodation was converted into a luxurious hotel.

Stranraer Swimming Gala, West Pier

This view of the old West Pier from the water gives an interesting perspective on its wooden structure. An additional row of young and more daring spectators has formed itself along the massive lower beams, an impressive indication of the numbers of people attending such events. A rowing boat attends the swimmers approaching the slipway. The *Free Press* of 1911 records that Lady Dalrymple fostered the swimming competition to encourage local boys' skills. Despite Stranraer's dominance of the short sea crossing, its development of harbour facilities came much later than those at other ports: until the late eighteenth century, the harbour was not much more than a natural anchorage, and at high tide ships could anchor close to the houses in Fisher Street. The West Pier was completed in 1820 after the Town Council experienced difficulties in raising the finance to built it. There were continuing problems thereafter in raising revenues from reluctant ship-owners to maintain it. The advent of the railways in 1861 provided the stimulus to the construction of the new East Pier, which laid the foundation for Stranraer's pre-eminence as the main mail and passenger port for Ireland.

Herring Boats with Drift Nets, Stranraer
A crowded quayside view of herring boats at Stranraer's old pier. The bow of the vessel jutting from the right belongs to a larger schooner, and one can only imagine the jostling and the skill required to disentangle an entire fleet when it left the port en masse. The webs of net hanging from the masts are drift-nets, which have been hung in the breeze to dry. Drift netting involved the suspension of long curtain of fine gill net, supported by round floats or *boughs*, in which the shoals of fish would become entrapped. By this time, the drift nets were made of cotton, which was much lighter than the old hempen nets, and therefore boats could carry many more nets, which would all be suspended together on a rope, or *fleet*. Drift-netting was suitable for those fish swimming relatively close to the surface and was used particularly for herring. Fishing for herring had a distinctive seasonal and daily rhythm and was carried out fairly close to the coast: the most intensive fishing was carried on from late July to mid-September, and fishing by drift-net was always carried out at night. The boats left in columns in late afternoon for the fishing grounds, shot and hauled their nets and returned by morning, racing to land their catch.

Stranraer: East Pier with Herring Boats, 1912

The East Pier was Stranraer's second pier, built in conjunction with the railway company, which eventually took it over in exchange for a rental and maintenance agreement with Stranraer Town Council. The herring boats in use here are the undecked types, which were capable of holding the large catches we can see here. These seem to be local boats, registered to Ballantrae. Wicker baskets on a pulley are used to hoist the catch to the quayside. The oars resting along the sides of the boats were used to assist sail-power when heading for harbour in an unfavourable wind.

Stranraer: Steam Drifters and Quay
The funnels of the steam drifters dominate the quay, where the landed cod has been laid out for sale. Steamships began to be used for drift-netting in 1898 on the east coast of Scotland, when the success of the herring industry warranted investment in the more expensive and powerful steam boats. It is notable that the registration numbers on the funnels indicate that the boats have come from the famous fishing towns of Banff and Fraserburgh. The scale of the herring industry in these towns has been well-documented by early photographers, such as George Washington Wilson, but the fleets also migrated widely in search of cod and haddock outside the three months of the summer herring fishery.

Herring being loaded into railway wagons, Stranraer
The proximity of the railway to the pier at Stranraer was critical to the whole process of landing the catch, curing, packing and shipping. Herring was highly perishable, and when a large catch arrived, the curers and packers had to work to capacity to treat the catch within twenty-four hours. The fish were gutted and packed in salt in barrels, which were left open (as on the left of the picture) for over a week while the brine settled. The intensity of the activity is indicated by the number of people employed in the different phases of packing and loading in this picture, and huge amounts of space were required on the docks for empty barrels, salt, open barrels still undergoing the curing process, and those ready to be loaded and shipped.

Redding Lines, Stranraer Pier

Fishing with a baited line was a traditional method with a long pedigree, and it survived alongside drift-netting. It was devised to catch *demersal* fish, such as cod or haddock, which live on or near the sea-bed. There were both *great* or *long* lines, which involved heavier lines and fewer hooks, and *small* lines, used for haddock, whiting and codling, which swim closer in to shore. The basic method was the same in both cases: a line, measuring hundreds of yards in length and marked on the surface by buoys, was laid close to the sea-bed and attached to this at intervals were shorter lengths of line with baited hooks. It looks as if the men here are preparing small-lines for haddock, and since this involved laying thousands of hooks at a time from one boat, one may imagine the time taken *redding* the lines. The preparation involved drying lines, baiting hooks, and stowing in trays so that the lines could be uncoiled without snagging. Although there two men are at work, it was often women who were deft at this form of on-shore work, as also at net-mending. Line-hauling at this time may have been carried out by steam-power, and later became powered by petrol, compressed air, or hydraulics.

Stranraer Fishermen, 1909

When this picture was taken on the old pier by Mr Ker, the Stranraer chemist, these men were working fishermen. Presumably, they are in their shore clothes, since they are more likely to have worn *ganseys* (guernseys), overalls, and long leather sea-boots, while at sea, though the caps probably remained the same. There are customs records referring to taxes on herring landed at Stranraer from as early as 1598, and the 1838 Statistical Account says that there had been *300 sail boats in the Loch at one time* fishing herring, perhaps encouraged by a Government bounty at this period of £3 per ton. The success of the industry appears to have fluctuated, but landings of fish at Stranraer reached a peak between 1900 and 1910 and showed a steady decline into the post World War II period. A report written in the 1950s documents there being sixty-five fishermen at Stranraer in the early twentieth century years, and that this had declined to only twenty in 1954.

Mission Ship, Loch Ryan
This unusual close-up shows the mission yacht which belonged to the Shipwrecked Mariners' Society which was founded in 1839. It cruised along the coasts in summer, addressing the spiritual needs and welfare of men in the Merchant Marine and their families. The vessel looks well-polished and her crew are equally smartly turned out, exuding the very air of late Victorian philanthropy. Even the harmonium has a waterproof cover, for the moments when either the seas or the rain threatened to disrupt the service. Presumably, the mission crew both went ashore to find congregations and also held services on board the ship. The *Wigtown Free Press* regularly records the holding of the Society's annual sermon.